The UK Breville Sandwich Maker Cookbook 2023

Kayleigh Scott

CONTENTS

INTRODUCTION

You've probably seen the commercials for the magical breakfast sandwich makers that, within five minutes or so, depending on the brand of sandwich maker, makes you a delicious breakfast sandwich that rivals the fast food joint with the golden arches. I hate making breakfast every morning, but I know how important it is and this gadget made it look so simple. So, my 12-year-old and I gave the breakfast sandwich maker a try.

How breakfast sandwich makers work
Using a breakfast sandwich maker is just as simple as the commercials make it look. You put a slice of bread in, add cheese and/or pre-cooked meat, slide the egg barrier in, crack an egg onto the egg barrier, top with another slice of bread and close.

Sandwiches in a snap
I tried the machine first and forgot to put the bread on top twice because I got distracted. This caused the egg to dribble out the side of the machine. No problem! The fantastic no-stick coating on the unit allowed me to wipe the egg off with one swipe of a towel. I was impressed.

Once I slowed down and used the machine like it was intended it was smooth sailing. The bread got properly toasted and the eggs cooked beautifully. My 12-year-old got the hang of using the sandwich maker on the first try.

I liked how the yolk stayed perfectly runny for those in our family that like runny yolks. For those that didn't like runny yolk, I simply scrambled the egg up with a fork a little bit after I dropped the egg in.

Timing is everything
What I didn't like is that there wasn't a reliable timer on the unit. It does have a preheat light, but as the manual says, this light doesn't indicate when the sandwich is done. Setting a kitchen timer to the suggested five minutes isn't a good remedy, either. We found that it can take anywhere from three to six minutes for a sandwich to cook, depending on the ingredients.

Eventually I found that it was best to just lift the lid up and take a peek every couple of minutes. This means you need to stick around and stay alert. It isn't an appliance you can set and leave to cook while you get ready for your day.

Don't smoosh
When using a panini maker, you may be used to squishing your sandwiches, but don't do that with a breakfast sandwich maker. Gently place the lid on top of your bread; it doesn't need to close completely to cook. If you do smoosh the lid down into place the egg with burst out of the appliance and will get all over your countertops.

Bread switch-up

All of the pictures on the box showed sandwiches made with round breads like bagels and English muffins, but we decided to give sliced loaf bread a try, too. You have to smash the edges of the bread into the unit just a bit, but it still came out perfectly toasted.

Cleaning up

Cleaning the breakfast sandwich maker is easy, too. Lifting the lid releases the sandwich making rings. They can be put in the dishwasher or can be washed by hand in hot, soapy water.

The plates on the unit can't be removed, but they can be wiped with a soapy sponge and then "rinsed" with a sponge damped with clean, warm water.

After you clean the unit, everything should be dried and coated with a non-stick cooking spray or wiped with vegetable oil to keep everything non-stick and tarnish-free.

Breakfast Sandwich Recipes

Sausage and Cheese

Ingredients:

- 1 buttermilk biscuit, sliced
- 1 maple pork sausage patty, cooked
- 1 slice cheddar cheese
- 1 large egg, beaten

Directions:

1. Preheat the breakfast sandwich maker.

2. Place half of the biscuit, cut-side up, inside the bottom tray of the sandwich maker.

3. Arrange the sausage patty on top of the biscuit and top with the slice of cheddar cheese.

4. Slide the egg tray into place and pour the beaten egg into it.

5. Top the egg with the other half of the biscuit.

6. Close the sandwich maker and cook for 4 to 5 minutes until the egg is cooked through.

7. Carefully rotate the egg tray out of the sandwich maker then open the sandwich maker and enjoy your sandwich.

Southwestern Breakfast Muffin

Ingredients:

- 1 whole wheat English muffin, split
- 2 tablespoons shredded hot pepper cheese
- 3 thin slices avocado
- 1 tablespoon salsa
- 2 large egg whites

Servings: 1

Cooking Time: 5 minutes

Directions:

1. Preheat Breakfast Sandwich Maker until green PREHEAT light comes on. Lift cover, top ring and cooking plate.
2. Place bottom half of English muffin, cut-side up in bottom ring of Breakfast Sandwich Maker. Top with cheese, avocado and salsa.
3. Lower cooking plate and top ring. Add egg whites to cooking plate.
4. Top with remaining muffin half, cut-side down.
5. Close cover. Cook 4 to 5 minutes.
6. Slide out cooking plate by rotating handle clockwise. Lift cover and rings; carefully remove sandwich with plastic spatula.

Reuben Sandwich

Ingredients:

- 2 slices rye bread or pumpernickel, cut in
- 4-inch circles
- 1 tablespoon softened butter
- 2 tablespoons thousand island dressing
- 3 slices corned beef, precooked
- 1/3 cup sauerkraut
- 1 slice Swiss cheese

Servings: 1

Cooking Time:
5 minutes

Directions:

1. Preheat Breakfast Sandwich Maker until green PREHEAT light comes on.
2. Butter one side of each bread circle. Spread dressing on other side of bread.
3. Lift cover, top ring and cooking plate. Place one bread circle, butter-side down in bottom ring of the breakfast sandwich maker. Top with cheese and sauerkraut.
4. Lower cooking plate and top ring. Add corned beef to cooking plate. Top with remaining bread circle, butter-side up.
5. Close cover. Cook 4 to 5 minutes.
6. Slide out cooking plate by rotating handle clockwise. Lift cover and rings; carefully remove sandwich with plastic spatula.

Protein Press English Muffin

Ingredients:

- 1 Thomas'® Light Multi-Grain English Muffin
- 1 slice Swiss cheese
- 2 slices cooked turkey bacon
- 1 large egg, lightly scrambled

Directions:

1. Preheat Breakfast Sandwich Maker until green PREHEAT light comes on.
2. Split Thomas'® Light Multi-Grain English Muffin in two. Lift cover, top ring and cooking plate. Place bottom half of the English muffin, split-side up in bottom ring of Breakfast Sandwich Maker. Top with cheese and precooked turkey bacon.
3. Lower cooking plate and top ring. Add egg to cooking plate. Top with remaining muffin half, splitside down.
4. Close cover. Cook 4 to 5 minutes.
5. Slide out cooking plate by rotating handle clockwise. Lift cover and rings; carefully remove sandwich with plastic spatula.

Stuffed French Toast

Ingredients:

- 1 large egg
- 1 large egg white
- 1 tablespoon cream cheese
- 1 tablespoon chopped pecans
- 2 slices cinnamon bread, cut in 4-inch circles
- 1 tablespoon strawberry preserves

Servings: 1

Cooking Time:
5 minutes

Directions:

1. Preheat Breakfast Sandwich Maker until green PREHEAT light comes on.

2. Beat egg and egg white in medium bowl; set aside.

3. Mix cream cheese and pecans in small bowl; spread on 1 slice of bread. Spread strawberry preserves on remaining bread slice. Make a sandwich placing filling sides together.

4. Place sandwich in egg mixture for 2 minutes; turn and soak for an additional 2 minutes.

5. Lift cover top ring and cooking plate. Place sandwich in bottom rimg of Breakfast Sandwich Maker.

6. Lower top ring and close cover. Cook 4 to 5 minutes or until cooked through.

7. Lift cover and rings; carefully remove sandwich with plastic spatula.

8. Serve with confectioners' sugar and additional preserves or maple syrup.

Monte Cristo Twist

Ingredients:

Servings: 1

Cooking Time: 5 minutes

- 2 slices frozen French toast
- 1 slices (1 ounce each) Swiss cheese
- 1 slice ham
- Maple syrup (optional)
- Powdered sugar (optional)

Directions:

1. Preheat breakfast sandwich maker. .
2. Place one slice French toast in bottom ring of breakfast sandwich maker. Top with 1 slice Swiss cheese, 1 slice ham, and 1 slice Brick cheese. .
3. Lower cooking plate and top ring. Top with remaining slice of French toast. .
4. Close cover. Cook 4 – 5 minutes. Gently rotate cooking plate handle away clockwise. Lift rings. Remove breakfast sandwich with a plastic or nylon spatula.
5. Sprinkle with powdered sugar. Serve with maple syrup.

Meat Lover's Biscuit

Ingredients:

- 1 buttermilk biscuit, sliced
- 2 slices Canadian bacon
- 1 pork sausage patty, cooked
- 1 slice deli ham
- 1 large egg

Servings: 1

Cooking Time: 5 minutes

Directions:

1. Preheat the breakfast sandwich maker.
2. Place half of the biscuit, cut-side up, inside the bottom tray of the sandwich maker.
3. Arrange the slices of Canadian bacon, sausage and ham on top of the biscuit half.
4. Slide the egg tray into place and crack the egg into it.
5. Top the egg with the other half of the biscuit.
6. Close the sandwich maker and cook for 4 to 5 minutes until the egg is cooked through.
7. Carefully rotate the egg tray out of the sandwich maker then open the sandwich maker and enjoy your sandwich.

Hash Browns and Sausage

Ingredients:

- 2 Hash brown patties
- 1 sausage patty, cooked
- 1 slice American cheese
- 1 large egg

Servings: 1

Cooking Time: 5 minutes

Directions:

1. Preheat breakfast sandwich maker.
2. Cook hash brown patties according to package directions.
3. Place one hash brown patty bottom ring of breakfast sandwich maker. Add sausage patty and American cheese.
4. Lower cooking plate and top ring. Add egg. Pierce top of egg with a toothpick or pointed plastic utensil.
5. Top egg with remaining hash brown patty.
6. Close cover. Cook 4 – 5 minutes. Gently rotate cooking plate handle away clockwise. Lift rings. Remove breakfast sandwich with a plastic or nylon spatula.

English Muffin Sandwich

Ingredients:

- 1 Thomas'® Original English Muffin
- 1 large egg
- 1 tablespoon chopped green bell pepper
- Salt and pepper, to taste
- 1 slice American cheese
- 2 slices cooked bacon

Directions:

1. Preheat Breakfast Sandwich Maker until green PREHEAT light comes on.

2. Split Thomas'® Original English Muffin in two. Lightly mix egg, milk, bell peppers, salt and pepper; set aside.

3. Lift cover, top ring and cooking plate. Place bottom half of the English muffin, split-side up in bottom ring of the Breakfast Sandwich Maker. Top with cheese and precooked bacon.

4. Lower cooking plate and top ring. Add egg mixture to cooking plate. Top with remaining muffin half, split-side down.

5. Close cover. Cook 4 to 5 minutes.

6. Slide out cooking plate by rotating handle clockwise. Lift cover and rings; carefully remove sandwich with plastic spatula.

Easy Ham and Scrambled Egg

Ingredients:

Servings: 1

Cooking Time: 5 minutes

- 2 slices whole grain bread
- 2 slices deli ham
- 1 slice Swiss cheese
- 1 large egg
- 2 teaspoons heavy cream
- 1 teaspoon chopped chives

Directions:

1. Preheat the breakfast sandwich maker.
2. Place one slice of bread in the bottom tray of the sandwich maker.
3. Arrange the slices of ham on top of the bread and top with the slice of Swiss cheese.
4. Beat together the egg, heavy cream and chives in a small bowl.
5. Slide the egg tray into place over the cheese and pour the beaten egg mixture into the tray.
6. Top the egg mixture with the remaining slice of bread.
7. Close the sandwich maker and cook for 4 to 5 minutes until the egg is cooked through.
8. Carefully rotate the egg tray out of the sandwich maker then open the sandwich maker and enjoy your sandwich.

Traditional BLT

Ingredients:

- 2 slices white bread
- 3 slices bacon, cooked
- 2 thin slices tomato
- 1 leaf Romaine lettuce, torn in half
- 2 teaspoons mayonnaise

Directions:

1. Spread one teaspoon of mayonnaise on each slice of bread.
2. Preheat the breakfast sandwich maker.
3. Place one slice of bread inside the bottom tray of the sandwich maker, mayonnaise-side facing up.
4. Break the slices of bacon in half and place them on top of the bread. Top with the slices of tomato.
5. Top the sandwich with the other slice of bread, mayonnaise-side down.
6. Close the sandwich maker and cook for 4 to 5 minutes.
7. Carefully open the sandwich maker and remove the top slice of bread.
8. Add the lettuce then replace the bread and enjoy your sandwich.

Vegetarian Panini Muffin

Ingredients:

- 1 Thomas'® High Fiber Triple Health English Muffin
- 1 tablespoon black olive tapenade or Kalamata
- olive spread
- 1 oz. slice fresh mozzarella
- 1 oz. roasted pepper
- 1 large egg white

Directions:

1. Preheat Breakfast Sandwich Maker until green PREHEAT light comes on.
2. Split Thomas'® High Fiber Triple Health English Muffin in two. Spread one half of muffin with tapenade; set aside.
3. Lift cover, top ring and cooking plate. Place half of the English muffin with tapenade side up in bottom ring of Breakfast Sandwich Maker.
4. Top with mozzarella and roasted pepper.
5. Lower cooking plate and top ring. Add egg to cooking plate. Top with remaining muffin half, splitside down.
6. Close cover. Cook 4 to 5 minutes.
7. Slide out cooking plate by rotating handle clockwise. Lift cover and rings; carefully remove sandwich with plastic spatula.

Classic Egg, Ham and Cheese

Ingredients:

Servings: 1

**Cooking Time:
5 minutes**

- 1 toasted English muffin, sliced
- 2 slices deli ham
- 1 slice cheddar cheese
- 1 large egg

Directions:

1. Preheat the breakfast sandwich maker.
2. Place half of the English muffin, cut-side up, inside the bottom tray of the sandwich maker.
3. Fold the slices of ham on top of the English muffin half and top with the slice of cheddar cheese.
4. Slide the egg tray into place and crack the egg into it.
5. Top the egg with the other half of the English muffin.
6. Close the sandwich maker and cook for 4 to 5 minutes until the egg is cooked through.
7. Carefully rotate the egg tray out of the sandwich maker then open the sandwich maker and enjoy your sandwich.

Canadian Bacon Bagel Sandwich

Ingredients:

Servings: 1

Cooking Time: 5 minutes

- 1 sesame seed bagel, cut in half
- 2 slices Canadian bacon
- 1 slice cheddar cheese
- 1 large egg

Directions:

1. Preheat the breakfast sandwich maker.
2. Place half of the bagel, cut-side up, inside the bottom tray of the sandwich maker.
3. Arrange the slices of Canadian bacon on top of the bagel and top with the slice of cheddar cheese.
4. Slide the egg tray into place and crack the egg into it.
5. Top the egg with the other half of the bagel.
6. Close the sandwich maker and cook for 4 to 5 minutes until the egg is cooked through.
7. Carefully rotate the egg tray out of the sandwich maker then open the sandwich maker and enjoy your sandwich.

Warm Chocolate Croissant

Ingredients:

- 1 mini croissant, halved
- 2 tablespoons chocolate hazelnut spread

Servings: 1

Cooking Time:
3 minutes

Directions:

1. Preheat Breakfast Sandwich Maker until green PREHEAT light comes on. Spread chocolate hazelnut spread over bottom half of croissant.
2. Lift cover, top ring and cooking plate.
3. Place bottom half of croissant, chocolate-side up in bottom ring of Breakfast Sandwich Maker.
4. Lower cooking plate and top ring. Place top half of croissant on cooking plate.
5. Close cover. Cook 2 to 3 minutes, just until chocolate and croissant are warm.
6. Slide out cooking plate by rotating handle clockwise. Lift cover and rings; carefully remove sandwich with plastic spatula.

Bacon, Egg & Cheese Bagel Sandwich

Ingredients:

- 1 small bagel, halved
- 1 slice American cheese
- 2 slices precooked bacon, cut in half
- 1 large egg, lightly scrambled

Directions:

1. Preheat Breakfast Sandwich Maker until green PREHEAT light comes on. Lift cover, top ring and cooking plate.

2. Place bottom half of bagel, cut-side up in bottom ring of Breakfast Sandwich Maker. Top with cheese and bacon.

3. Lower cooking plate and top ring. Add egg to cooking plate.

4. Top with remaining bagel half, cut-side down.

5. Close cover. Cook 4 to 5 minutes.

6. Slide out cooking plate by rotating handle clockwise. Lift cover and rings; carefully remove sandwich with plastic spatula.

Hash Brown Sausage Sandwich

Ingredients:

- 2 frozen hash brown patties
- 1 turkey sausage patty
- 1 slice cheddar cheese
- 1 large egg, beaten

Servings: 1

Cooking Time: 5 minutes

Directions:

1. Heat the butter in a small skillet over medium heat. Add the hash brown patties and cook until lightly browned on one side.

2. Flip the patties and cook until browned on the other side.

3. Preheat the breakfast sandwich maker.

4. Place one of the hash brown patties inside the bottom ring of the sandwich maker.

5. Top the hash brown with the sausage patty and slice of cheddar cheese.

6. Slide the egg tray into place and crack the egg into it.

7. Top the egg with the other hash brown patty.

8. Close the sandwich maker and cook for 4 to 5 minutes until the egg is cooked through.

9. Carefully rotate the egg tray out of the sandwich maker then open the sandwich maker and enjoy your sandwich.

Grilled Cheese Sandwich

Ingredients:

- 2 slices bread, cut in 4-inch circles
- Butter, softened
- 2 slices American cheese

Directions:

1. Preheat Breakfast Sandwich Maker until green PREHEAT light comes on. Lightly butter one side of each bread circle. Lift cover, top ring and cooking plate.

2. Place one bread circle, buttered-side down in bottom ring of Breakfast Sandwich Maker. Top with cheese.

3. Lower cooking plate and top ring. Add bread circle, buttered-side up on cooking plate.

4. Close cover. Cook 3 to 4 minutes.

5. Slide out cooking plate by rotating handle clockwise. Lift cover and rings; carefully remove sandwich with plastic spatula.

Fruit Breakfast Sandwich Recipes

Grilled mixed nuts sandwich

Ingredients:

- 4 slices whole-wheat bread
- ½ tsp light butter
- ¼ cup roasted mixed nuts (almonds, pecans, walnuts, cashews, etc.)
- 1 tbsp wild honey

Directions:

1. Lightly pat butter on each sandwich maker pan.
2. Mix together the mixed nuts and honey.
3. Make two sandwiches with the honeyed mixed nuts.
4. Cook in sandwich maker for about 3 minutes.
5. Serve hot.

Grilled baklava sandwich

Ingredients:

- 4 slices whole-wheat bread
- ½ tsp light butter
- ¼ cup pistachios, crushed
- 2 tsp wild honey
- ½ tsp ground cinnamon

Directions:

1. Lightly pat butter on each sandwich maker pan.
2. Mix together the pistachios, wild honey, and cinnamon.
3. Make two sandwiches with the pistachio mixture.
4. Cook in sandwich maker for about 3 minutes.
5. Serve hot.

Warm fruit cocktail sandwich

Ingredients:

Servings: 2

Cooking Time: 3 minutes

- 4 slices whole-wheat bread
- ½ tsp light butter
- 1 cup canned unsweetened fruit cocktail mix, drained

Directions:

1. Lightly pat butter on preheated sandwich maker.
2. Place two bread slices on the sandwich maker.
3. Distribute fruit cocktail and light sprinkles of its syrup if desired.
4. Top with remaining bread slices.
5. Cook in sandwich maker for about 3 minutes.
6. Serve hot.

Chocolate Raspberry Croissant

Ingredients:

Servings: 1

Cooking Time: 5 minutes

- 1 croissant, sliced
- 2 tbsp. chocolate hazelnut spread
- ½ cup fresh raspberries
- 2 tbsp. crème fraiche

Directions:

1. Brush 1 tbsp. chocolate hazelnut spread on each half of the croissant.
2. Preheat the breakfast sandwich maker.
3. Place half of the croissant, cut-side up, inside the bottom tray of the sandwich maker.
4. Top the croissant with the raspberries and crème fraiche.
5. Place the second half of the croissant on top of the raspberries.
6. Close the sandwich maker and cook for 4 to 5 minutes until heated through.
7. Carefully open the sandwich maker and enjoy your sandwich.

Cranberry Bagel Sausage Treat

Ingredients:

- 1 sausage patty, fully cooked
- 1 large egg
- 1 small cranberry bagel, split
- 1 tablespoons cream cheese
- 1 teaspoon chopped green onions or chives
- Cranberry chutney (optional)

Directions:

1. Preheat breakfast sandwich maker.
2. Spread cut side of bagel halves with cream cheese
3. Place one-half bagel, spread side up, into bottom ring of breakfast sandwich maker. Add cooked sausage patty.
4. Lower cooking plate and top ring. Add egg. Pierce top of egg with a toothpick or pointed plastic utensil.
5. Sprinkle egg with chopped chives or green onion. Top with remaining bagel half, spread side down.
6. Close cover. Cook 4 – 5 minutes. Gently rotate cooking plate handle away clockwise. Lift rings. Remove breakfast sandwich with a nylon spatula.
7. Optional: dip sandwich in cranberry chutney.

Apricot and Brie Croissant

Ingredients:

Servings: 1

Cooking Time:
5 minutes

- 1 medium croissant
- ½ teaspoon of dark brown sugar
- Cinnamon to taste
- 1 ounce of brie, cut into slices, rind removed
- ½ tablespoon of chopped, glazed pecans
- 1 tablespoon of apricot preserves

Directions:

1. Preheat the sandwich maker, so it can be warming while you prepare the rest of the sandwich.
2. Slice the croissant.
3. Take the bottom of the croissant and cover it with the brie.
4. Spread the apricot preserves on top of the cheese.
5. Place the croissant bottom in the bottom slot of the sandwich maker, topping with the pecans and the dark brown sugar.
6. Sprinkle with a bit of cinnamon.
7. Put the top of the croissant into the top slot of the appliance.
8. Allow to cook for about 5 minutes, ensuring that the croissant is nicely browned.
9. Remove sandwich and eat while still warm.

Cherry pineapple cake-wich

Ingredients:

- 4 slices whole-wheat bread
- ½ tsp light butter
- ½ cup canned unsweetened pineapple chunks, drained
- ¼ cup cherries, slightly crushed.

Directions:

1. Lightly pat butter on each sandwich maker pan.
2. Make two sandwiches with layers of pineapples and cherries, and light sprinkles of pineapple syrup if desired.
3. Cook in sandwich maker for about 3 minutes.
4. Serve hot.

Peanut Butter Banana Sandwich

Ingredients:

- 2 slices white bread
- 2 tbsp. smooth peanut butter
- 1 large banana, sliced

Directions:

1. Preheat the breakfast sandwich maker.
2. Place one slice of bread, already coated with peanut butter, side up inside the bottom tray of the sandwich maker.
3. Top the bread with slices of banana.
4. Place the second piece of bread on top of the banana.
5. Close the sandwich maker and cook for 4 to 5 minutes until heated through.
6. Carefully open the sandwich maker and enjoy your sandwich.

Bacon, Avocado and Cheddar

Ingredients:

- 2 slices multi-grain bread, cut into rounds
- 2 slices thick cut bacon, cooked
- 1 slice sharp cheddar
- 1/4 Avocado, sliced
- 1 slice red onion
- 1 Tbsp Aioli
- 1 large egg

Directions:

1. Preheat breakfast sandwich maker.
2. Place slice of whole grain bread, into bottom ring of breakfast sandwich maker. Add bacon, sharp cheddar cheese, avocado slices and red onion.
3. Lower cooking plate and top ring. Add egg. Pierce top of egg with a toothpick or pointed plastic utensil.
4. Spread remaining slice of bread with Aioli (or other favorite topping). Place spread side down on top of egg.
5. Close cover. Cook 4 – 5 minutes. Gently rotate cooking plate handle away clockwise. Lift rings. Remove breakfast sandwich with a plastic or nylon spatula.

Ricotta Basil Biscuit with Nectarines

Ingredients:

- 1 buttermilk biscuit, sliced
- 1 ripe nectarine, peeled and sliced
- 1 tbsp. ricotta cheese
- 1 tbsp. maple syrup
- 2 tsp. brown sugar

Servings: 1

Cooking Time:
5 minutes

Directions:

1. Place the nectarines in a bowl and add the ricotta, maple syrup and brown sugar then toss well.
2. Preheat the breakfast sandwich maker.
3. Place half of the biscuit, cut-side up, inside the bottom tray of the sandwich maker.
4. Top the muffin with the nectarine slices, ricotta, maple syrup and brown sugar mixture
5. Place the second half of the biscuit on top of the nectarines.
6. Close the sandwich maker and cook for 4 to 5 minutes until heated through.
7. Carefully open the sandwich maker and enjoy your sandwich.

Eggs Breakfast Sandwich Recipes

Fried Egg and Cheese Bagel

Ingredients:

- 1 plain bagel, sliced
- 1 egg
- 1 pat of butter
- 1 slice of American cheese
- Ketchup to taste (optional)

Directions:

1. Preheat your sandwich maker until it is ready.
2. Take the bottom of the sliced bagel, placing it in the bottom ring of the sandwich maker.
3. Place the slice of American cheese on top of the bagel bottom.
4. In the egg slot, place a tiny pat of butter and then crack an egg onto the cooking plate.
5. In the top slot, add the top of the bagel.
6. Close the appliance and cook until eggs reach your desired consistency. If you like the yolks hard, cook for about five minutes. If you want your fried egg over easy, then reduce cooking time by a minute or so.
7. Slip out the cooking plate, then carefully open and remove the sandwich.
8. Eat immediately.

Eggs Parmesan English Muffin

Ingredients:

- 1 English muffin (whole grain is best), split
- 1 large egg
- 1/8 cup of parmesan cheese
- 1/4 cup of marinara sauce

Servings: 1

Cooking Time:
5 minutes

Directions:

1. Begin by preheating the breakfast sandwich maker until the ready light comes on.
2. When the appliance is ready, open and add the bottom of the English muffin to the bottom slot.
3. Top the bottom of the English muffin with the cup of marinara sauce.
4. Sprinkle the cup of parmesan cheese on top of the sauce.
5. Next, add the egg to the cooking plate.
6. Add the top of the English muffin to the top slot.
7. Close and cook for 4-5 minutes, giving the egg time to cook and the sauce and cheese time to warm.
8. Remove the cooking plate and then open the appliance, taking the sandwich out carefully.
9. Enjoy the sandwich while hot.

Green Eggs and Ham

Ingredients:

- 1 English muffin
- 1/2 cup baby spinach, washed and chopped
- 1 tsp olive oil
- 1 slice Cheddar cheese
- 1 slice ham
- 1 egg
- Fresh basil (optional)

Servings: 1

Cooking Time:
5 minutes

Directions:

1. Preheat breakfast sandwich maker.
2. Place one-half muffin, split side up, into bottom ring of breakfast sandwich maker. Add 1 slice each of Ham and Cheddar cheese.
3. In small sauté pan heat olive oil. Add spinach and sauté until just softened. Remove from heat.
4. In small bowl, blend spinach and egg together with a fork.
5. Lower cooking plate and top ring. Add egg and spinach mixture.
6. Top with remaining muffin half, split side down.
7. Close cover. Cook 4 – 5 minutes. Gently rotate cooking plate handle away clockwise. Lift rings. Remove breakfast sandwich with a plastic or nylon spatula.

Chorizo Egg Torta

Ingredients:

- 1 round flatbread, sliced crosswise
- 1 Chorizo Sausage patty, cooked
- 1/2 Avocado, cleaned, pitted and sliced
- 2 ounces Monterey Jack, shredded
- 1 Tbsp Feta cheese or Queso Fresco, crumbled
- 1 large egg

Servings: 1

Cooking Time: 5 minutes

Directions:

1. Preheat breakfast sandwich maker.
2. Place the bottom slice of flatbread, split side up, into bottom ring of breakfast sandwich maker. Add Chorizo sausage patty. Add Avocado slices, Monterey Jack and Feta to top of sausage.
3. In small bowl, gently whisk egg.
4. Lower cooking plate and top ring.
5. Add whisked egg to cooking plate. Top with remaining flatbread slice, split side down.
6. Close cover. Cook 4 – 5 minutes. Gently rotate cooking plate handle away clockwise. Lift rings. Remove breakfast sandwich with a plastic or nylon spatula.

Muffuletta Egg Sandwich

Ingredients:

Servings: 1

**Cooking Time:
5 minutes**

- 1 slice ham, cooked
- 1 egg
- 2 slices French bread
- 1 slice provolone cheese
- 1 tbsp pimento-stuffed green olives, chopped
- 1 tbsp roasted red bell pepper, drained and chopped

Directions:

1. Preheat breakfast sandwich maker.
2. Place one slice of French bread into bottom ring of breakfast sandwich maker. Add ham slice. Sprinkle pimentos and peppers over ham. Top with provolone cheese slice.
3. Lower cooking plate and top ring. Add egg. Pierce top of egg with a toothpick or pointed plastic utensil.
4. Top with remaining French bread slice.
5. Close cover. Cook 4 – 5 minutes. Gently rotate cooking plate handle away clockwise. Lift rings. Remove breakfast sandwich with nylon spatula.

Buttermilk Biscuit with Eggs

Ingredients:

- 1 buttermilk biscuit, cut in half
- 1 slice of sharp cheddar cheese
- 1 egg
- Milk
- Salt and pepper to taste

Directions:

1. In a bowl, crack the egg and add a bit of milk. Add a dash of salt and pepper for flavor. Use a whisk to whisk the egg and milk together.
2. Make sure the breakfast sandwich maker is preheated.
3. Take the bottom of the biscuit, placing it in the bottom slot of the breakfast sandwich maker.
4. Top the bottom of the biscuit with the slice of cheddar cheese.
5. Pour the egg mixture into the egg slot.
6. Place the biscuit top in the top slot of the sandwich maker.
7. Close and cook for about five minutes.
8. Remove cooking plate, open the appliance and carefully take out the sandwich.
9. Remove the top of the biscuit and add ketchup if desired.
10. Enjoy while warm.

Easy Bread Pudding Sandwich

Ingredients:

Servings: 1

Cooking Time: 5 minutes

- 2 slices stale bread, cubed
- 1 large egg
- 2 tbsp. maple syrup or honey
- 2 tbsp. plain yogurt
- 1 tbsp. melted butter
- Pinch ground nutmeg
- 1 chicken sausage patty, cooked
- 1 slice Swiss cheese
- 1 large egg

Directions:

1. Arrange the chunks of bread in a small round ramekin.
2. Whisk together the remaining ingredients and pour over the bread – do not stir.
3. Microwave the ramekin on high heat for 2 minutes until the pudding is firm and hot. Let cool for 5 minutes.
4. Preheat the breakfast sandwich maker.
5. Turn the bread pudding out of the ramekin and into the bottom of the breakfast sandwich maker.
6. Top the bread pudding with the sausage patty and slice of Swiss cheese.
7. Slide the egg tray into place and crack the egg into it. Use a fork to stir the egg, just breaking the yolk.
8. Close the sandwich maker and cook for 4 to 5 minutes until the egg is cooked through.
9. Carefully rotate the egg tray out of the sandwich maker then open the sandwich maker to enjoy your sandwich.

Meat Breakfast Sandwich Recipes

Pepperoni pizza-wich

Ingredients:

- 2 tortillas
- 1 tsp olive oil
- 8-12 pepperoni slices
- ½ cup part-skim mozzarella cheese, shredded
- ¼ cup tomato paste
- 1 tsp dried herbs of choice (oregano, basil, rosemary, thyme, etc.)

Directions:

1. Lightly pat olive oil on each sandwich maker pan.
2. Lightly spread olive oil and then tomato paste on one side of each tortilla.
3. Make tortilla folds, layering the other ingredients.
4. Cook in sandwich maker for about 3 minutes.
5. Serve hot.

Servings: 2

Cooking Time:
3 minutes

Pepper Jack Sausage Sandwich

Ingredients:

- 1 buttermilk biscuit, sliced in half
- 1 tsp. horseradish sauce
- 1 pork sausage patty, cooked
- 1 slice Pepper Jack cheese
- 1 large egg, beaten

Servings: 1

Cooking Time: 5 minutes

Directions:

1. Spread the horseradish sauce on the bottom half of the biscuit.
2. Preheat the breakfast sandwich maker.
3. Place the bottom half of the biscuit, cut-side up, inside the bottom tray of the sandwich maker.
4. Top the biscuit with the sausage patty and Pepper Jack cheese.
5. Slide the egg tray into place and pour the beaten egg into it.
6. Place the second half of the biscuit on top of the egg.
7. Close the sandwich maker and cook for 4 to 5 minutes until the egg is cooked through.
8. Carefully rotate the egg tray out of the sandwich maker then open the sandwich maker to enjoy your sandwich.

Grilled spaghetti bites

Ingredients:

- 4 slices whole-wheat bread
- ½ tsp olive oil
- ½ cup spaghetti, cooked or leftover
- 8 strips extra-lean turkey bacon, defrosted
- 1 tbsp Parmesan cheese, grated (optional)

Directions:

1. Lightly pat oil on each sandwich maker pan.
2. Place two bread slices on the sandwich maker.
3. Top with spaghetti and cheese.
4. Top with the two remaining bread slices.
5. Cook in sandwich maker for about 3 minutes.
6. Serve hot.

Servings: 2

Cooking Time:
3 minutes

Greek chicken feta grill

Ingredients:

- 4 slices whole-wheat bread
- 1 tsp olive oil
- ½ cup canned chicken breast in water, sliced into chunks
- ½ cup light feta cheese
- 1 clove garlic, chopped
- ¼ cup onions, chopped
- 1 tsp capers, chopped
- 1 tbsp lemon juice

Servings: 2

Cooking Time: 5 minutes

Directions:

1. Lightly pat olive oil on each sandwich maker pan.
2. Mix together the chicken and other ingredients.
3. Make two sandwiches with the chicken mixture.
4. Cook in sandwich maker for about 5 minutes.
5. Serve hot.

Cranberry turkey sandwich grill

Ingredients:

Servings: 2

Cooking Time: 3 minutes

- 4 slices whole-wheat bread
- ½ tsp olive oil
- 8 strips cooked turkey breast
- 2 tbsp cranberry sauce
- ¼ cup fresh spinach leaves

Directions:

1. Lightly pat olive oil on each sandwich maker pan.
2. Make two sandwiches, spreading the cranberry sauce and topping with turkey strips and spinach.
3. Cook in sandwich maker for about 3 minutes.
4. Serve hot.

Creamy egg sandwich grill

Ingredients:

Servings: 2

Cooking Time: 3 minutes

- 4 slices whole-wheat bread
- ½ tsp light butter
- 1 large egg, hard-boiled and slightly mashed
- ½ onion, chopped
- 2 tbsp light mayonnaise

Directions:

1. Lightly pat butter on each sandwich maker pan.
2. Mix together in a bowl the egg, light mayonnaise, and onions.
3. Make two sandwiches with the egg mixture.
4. Cook in sandwich maker for about 3 minutes.
5. Serve hot.

Rustic Ham and Cheese Sandwich

Ingredients:

- 2 slices (1/2-inch thick) Rustic white country bread
- 1 slices (1 ounce) Wisconsin Gruyere or Swiss cheese
- 2 Jones Ham Slices
- 1 slice, (1 ounce) Wisconsin Brick cheese
- 1 egg
- 1 tablespoon fresh Rosemary, chopped (optional)

Directions:

1. Preheat breakfast sandwich maker.
2. Place one slice rustic white bread in bottom ring of breakfast sandwich maker. Top with 1 slice Gruyere cheese and 2 slices ham. Sprinkle lightly with fresh chopped rosemary. Top with 1 slice Brick cheese.
3. Lower cooking plate and top ring. Add egg to top of ring and pierce yolk. Sprinkle fresh rosemary on top of egg. Top with remaining slice of rustic white bread.
4. Close cover. Cook 4 – 5 minutes. Gently rotate cooking plate handle away clockwise. Lift rings. Remove breakfast sandwich with a plastic or nylon spatula.

Chipotle Chicken Sandwich

Ingredients:

- 1 ciabatta roll, sliced
- 1 cooked chicken patty
- 1 slice Pepper Jack cheese
- 1 tbsp. chipotle mayonnaise
- 1 large egg
- 1 slice red onion
- 1 piece romaine lettuce, torn in half

Directions:

1. Preheat the breakfast sandwich maker.
2. Place half of the ciabatta roll, cut-side up, inside the bottom tray of the sandwich maker.
3. Top the ciabatta with the chicken patty and Pepper Jack cheese.
4. Slide the egg tray into place and crack the egg into it. Use a fork to stir the egg, just breaking the yolk.
5. Brush the other half of the ciabatta roll with the chipotle mayonnaise.
6. Place the second half of the ciabatta on top of the egg.
7. Close the sandwich maker and cook for 4 to 5 minutes until the egg is cooked through.
8. Carefully rotate the egg tray out of the sandwich maker then open the sandwich maker.
9. Remove the top ciabatta roll and top the sandwich with the onion and lettuce. Replace the roll to enjoy the sandwich.

Southwestern Chicken Sandwich

Ingredients:

Servings: 1

Cooking Time: 5 minutes

- 1 croissant, sliced
- 1 Applegate Farms natural chicken patty, cooked
- 1 slice Monterey Jack cheese
- 1 tbsp Chipotle mayo
- 1 large egg
- Arugula (optional)
- Tomato slice (optional)
- Red onion slice (optional)

Directions:

1. Preheat breakfast sandwich maker.

2. Place bottom half of croissant, split side up, into bottom ring of breakfast sandwich maker. Add cooked chicken patty – we used Applegate Farms patties, but any good crispy natural chicken patty will work. Top with Monterey Jack.

3. In small bowl, gently whisk egg.

4. Lower cooking plate and top ring.

5. Add whisked egg to cooking plate. Top with tomato slice, Arugula and red onion slice if desired.

6. Spread Chipotle mayo on top slice of croissant. Place croissant, spread side down on top of egg.

7. Close cover. Cook 4 – 5 minutes. Gently rotate cooking plate handle away clockwise. Lift rings. Remove breakfast sandwich with a nylon spatula.

Cheesy bacon grill

Ingredients:

- 4 slices whole-wheat bread
- ½ tsp light butter
- 8 strips extra-lean turkey bacon
- ¼ cup onions, chopped
- ½ cup part-skim mozzarella cheese, shredded

Servings: 2

Cooking Time: 5 minutes

Directions:

1. Lightly pat butter on each sandwich maker pan.
2. Make two sandwiches, layering the turkey bacon, cheese, and onions.
3. Cook in sandwich maker for about 5 minutes.
4. Serve hot.

Tuna nicoise salad-wich

Ingredients:

- 4 slices whole-wheat bread
- 1 tsp olive oil
- 1 can tuna chunks in water, drained
- 1 medium egg, hard-boiled, sliced
- ¼ cup tomatoes, diced
- ¼ cup fresh basil leaves
- 2 tbsp white wine vinegar

Servings: 2

Cooking Time: 5 minutes

Directions:

1. Lightly pat olive oil on each sandwich maker pan.
2. Mix together tuna, tomatoes, olive oil, and white wine vinegar.
3. Make two sandwiches with tuna mixture, egg slices and basil leaves.
4. Cook in sandwich maker for about 3 minutes.
5. Serve hot.

Aloha pizza-wich

Ingredients:

- 2 whole-wheat tortillas
- ½ tsp olive oil
- 2 slices extra lean ham
- 2 slices canned unsweetened pineapple rings
- ½ cup part-skim mozzarella cheese, shredded
- 1 tsp dried herbs of choice (oregano, basil, rosemary, thyme, etc.)

Servings: 2

Cooking Time: 5 minutes

Directions:

1. Lightly pat olive oil on each sandwich maker pan.
2. Make tortilla folds, layering each filling ingredient.
3. Cook in sandwich maker for about 5 minutes.
4. Serve hot.

Turkey Cobb Sandwich

Ingredients:

- 1 sandwich bun, medium
- 3 oz deli turkey breast slices
- 2 slices bacon, cooked
- 1/4 avocado, sliced
- 2 oz blue cheese
- 1 egg

Servings: 1

Cooking Time: 5 minutes

Directions:

1. Preheat breakfast sandwich maker.
2. Place lower half of bun into bottom ring of breakfast sandwich maker. Add turkey breast, bacon (large crumbles), avocado and blue cheese.
3. Lower cooking plate and top ring. Add egg. Pierce top of egg with a toothpick or pointed plastic utensil. Top with top of bun.
4. Close cover. Cook 4 – 5 minutes. Gently rotate cooking plate handle away clockwise. Lift rings. Remove sandwich with a spatula.

Vegetarian Breakfast Sandwich Recipes

Guacamole sandwich grill

Ingredients:

- 4 pcs whole-wheat pita bread
- ½ tsp olive oil
- ½ cup avocado, mashed
- ¼ cup tomatoes, diced
- ¼ cup onions, chopped
- 1 tsp lime juice

Directions:

1. Lightly pat olive oil on each sandwich maker pan.
2. For the guacamole, mix together the avocado, tomatoes, onions, and lime juice.
3. Make four pita folds with the guacamole.
4. Cook in sandwich maker for about 3 minutes.
5. Serve hot.

Grilled mushroom swiss

Ingredients:

- 4 slices whole-wheat bread
- ½ tsp light butter
- ¼ cup cooked white button mushrooms, sliced or crushed
- 2 slices light Swiss cheese

Directions:

1. Lightly pat butter on each sandwich maker pan.
2. Place the breads on the sandwich maker
3. Place one slice of cheese on each bread and top with mushrooms.
4. Top with the two remaining breads.
5. Cook in sandwich maker for about 3 minutes.
6. Serve hot.

Margherita pizza-wich

Ingredients:

Servings: 2

Cooking Time: 3 minutes

- 2 whole-wheat tortillas
- 1 tsp olive oil
- 2 slices part-skim mozzarella cheese
- 1 medium tomato, sliced
- ½ cup fresh basil leaves, chopped
- 1 clove garlic, chopped

Directions:

1. Lightly pat olive oil on each sandwich maker pan.
2. Lightly brush olive oil on one side of each tortilla.
3. Make tortilla folds, layering each filling ingredient.
4. Cook in sandwich maker for about 3 minutes.
5. Serve hot.

Grilled hummus sandwich

Ingredients:

Servings: 2

Cooking Time: 3 minutes

- 4 pcs whole-wheat pita bread
- ½ tsp olive oil
- 2 tbsp hummus
- ¼ cup tomatoes, diced
- ¼ cup onions, chopped

Directions:

1. Lightly pat olive oil on each sandwich maker pan.
2. Mix together in a bowl the hummus, onions and tomatoes.
3. Make four pita folds with hummus mixture.
4. Cook in sandwich maker for about 3 minutes.
5. Serve hot.

Florentine Eggs

Ingredients:

- 1/8 cup plain yogurt
- 1/4 teaspoon Dijon mustard
- 1 egg
- 1/2 English muffin
- 1/4 cup fresh baby spinach leaves
- Salt and pepper to taste

Servings: 1

Cooking Time:
5 minutes

Directions:

1. Preheat breakfast sandwich maker.
2. Mix yogurt and mustard together. Spread on English muffin half.
3. Place muffin, yogurt side up, into bottom ring of breakfast sandwich maker. Add baby spinach leaves.
4. Lower cooking plate and top ring. Add egg. Pierce top of egg with a toothpick or pointed plastic utensil.
5. Close cover. Cook 4 – 5 minutes. Gently rotate cooking plate handle away clockwise. Lift rings. Remove breakfast sandwich with a plastic or nylon spatula.
6. Season to taste with salt and pepper.

Fat-Burning Breakfast Sandwich

Ingredients:

Servings: 1

Cooking Time: 5 minutes

- ½ toasted whole grain English muffin
- 2 tsp. olive oil
- ¼ ripe Avocado
- 1 slice Swiss cheese
- 1 slice tomato
- 1 egg,

Directions:

1. Preheat breakfast sandwich maker.
2. Drizzle olive oil over the English muffin. Place muffin into bottom ring of breakfast sandwich maker. Add the avocado, Swiss cheese and tomato.
3. Lower cooking plate and top ring. Add egg. Pierce top of egg with a toothpick or pointed plastic utensil. Sprinkle with pepper, if desired.
4. Close cover. Cook 4 – 5 minutes. Gently rotate cooking plate handle away clockwise. Lift rings. Remove breakfast sandwich with a plastic or nylon spatula.

Egg and Cheddar Cheese Biscuit

Ingredients:

- 1 biscuit, sliced
- 1 slice cheddar cheese
- 1 slice red onion
- 1 slice green pepper, seeded and cored
- 1 large egg

Directions:

1. Preheat the breakfast sandwich maker.

2. Place half of the biscuit, cut-side up, inside the bottom tray of the sandwich maker.

3. Top the biscuit with a slice of cheddar cheese along with the red onion and green pepper.

4. Slide the egg tray into place and crack the egg into it.

5. Top the egg with the other half of the biscuit.

6. Close the sandwich maker and cook for 4 to 5 minutes until the egg is cooked through.

7. Carefully rotate the egg tray out of the sandwich maker then open the sandwich maker and enjoy your sandwich.

Cinnamon Raisin Apple Sandwich

Ingredients:

Servings: 1

Cooking Time: 5 minutes

- 2 slices cinnamon raisin bread
- ½ small apple, sliced thin
- 1 thin slice cheddar cheese
- ½ teaspoon unsalted butter
- Pinch ground cinnamon and nutmeg

Directions:

1. Preheat the breakfast sandwich maker.
2. Place one slice of bread inside the bottom tray of the sandwich maker. Spread the bread with butter.
3. Top the bread with the slices of apple then sprinkle them with cinnamon and nutmeg.
4. Place the slice of cheddar cheese over the apples. Top the cheese with the other piece of bread.
5. Close the sandwich maker and cook for 4 to 5 minutes until it is heated through.
6. Carefully open the sandwich maker and enjoy your sandwich.

Sandwich maker quesadilla

Ingredients:

Servings: 2

Cooking Time:
3 minutes

- 2 whole-wheat tortillas
- ½ tsp light butter
- ½ cup reduced-fat cheddar cheese, grated
- ¼ cup tomatoes, diced
- ¼ cup onions, chopped

Directions:

1. Lightly pat butter on each sandwich maker pan.
2. Place the tortillas on the sandwich maker.
3. Equally distribute cheese, and scatter tomatoes and onions on half of both tortillas.
4. Fold the tortillas.
5. Cook in sandwich maker for about 3 minutes.
6. Serve hot.

Cheesy broccoli sandwich

Ingredients:

Servings: 2

Cooking Time:
5 minutes

- 4 slices whole-wheat bread
- ½ tsp light butter
- ½ cup broccoli flowers, sliced
- ½ cup reduced-fat cheddar cheese, shredded

Directions:

1. Lightly pat butter on each sandwich maker pan.
2. Make two sandwiches, layering the broccoli and cheese.
3. Cook in sandwich maker for about 3-5 minutes.
4. Serve hot.

Sandwich maker spinach calzone

Ingredients:

Servings: 2

Cooking Time: 3 minutes

- 4 slices whole-wheat bread
- ½ tsp olive oil
- ½ cup fresh spinach
- ¼ cup tomatoes, diced
- ½ cup part-skim mozzarella cheese, shredded
- ¼ cup fat-free ricotta cheese

Directions:

1. Lightly pat olive oil on each sandwich maker pan.
2. Mix together in a bowl the spinach, tomatoes, and cheeses.
3. Make two sandwiches with the spinach mixture.
4. Cook in the sandwich maker for about 3 minutes.
5. Serve hot.

Baked beans sandwich grill

Ingredients:

Servings: 2

Cooking Time: 3 minutes

- 4 slices whole-wheat bread
- ½ tsp light butter
- ½ cup canned low sodium baked beans

Directions:

1. Lightly pat butter on each sandwich maker pan.
2. Place the bread slices on the sandwich maker pan.
3. Spread the baked beans on the bread slices.
4. Top with the remaining bread slices.
5. Cook in sandwich maker for about 3 minutes.
6. Serve hot.

Tomato Basil Flatbread

Ingredients:

Servings: 1

Cooking Time: 5 minutes

- 1 small round flatbread
- 1 tsp. olive oil
- Salt and pepper to taste
- 1 thick slice ripe tomato
- 4 fresh basil leaves
- 1 slice fresh mozzarella cheese
- 1 large egg

Directions:

1. Preheat the breakfast sandwich maker.
2. Place the round flatbread inside the bottom tray of the sandwich maker.
3. Brush the flatbread with the olive oil and sprinkle with salt and pepper.
4. Top the flatbread with the slice of tomato, basil leaves and mozzarella cheese.
5. Slide the egg tray into place and crack the egg into it. Use a fork to stir the egg, just breaking the yolk. Close the sandwich maker and cook for 4 to 5 minutes until the egg is cooked through
6. Carefully rotate the egg tray out of the sandwich maker then open the sandwich maker to enjoy your sandwich.

Cheesy carrot and cucumber sandwich

Ingredients:

- 4 slices whole-wheat bread
- ½ tsp light butter
- 1 small carrot, sliced into thin circles
- ½ cucumber, sliced into circles
- 2 slices reduced-fat cheddar cheese

Servings: 2

Cooking Time: 5 minutes

Directions:

1. Lightly pat butter on each sandwich maker pan.
2. Make two sandwiches, layering the carrots, cheese, and cucumber.
3. Cook in sandwich maker for about 3-5 minutes.
4. Serve hot.

Dates, Goat Cheese Vegetarian Bagel

Ingredients:

- 2 multigrain bagels, sliced
- ½ cup of rinsed arugula leaves, carefully dried
- 3 tablespoons of goat cheese
- ½ cup of chopped walnuts
- 8 dates, pitted and thinly sliced

Directions:

1. Preheat the sandwich maker.
2. Take the bottom of one bagel, spreading it with half of the goat cheese. Place into the bottom slot of the appliance.
3. Sprinkle with half of the walnuts, topping the walnuts with half of the thinly sliced dates.
4. In the top slot, place the other half of the multigrain bagel.
5. Cook the sandwich for three minutes. Remove carefully.
6. Take off the top of the sandwich, adding half of the arugula leaves and then putting the top back on.
7. Repeat the process with the second multigrain bagel.
8. Eat warm.

Waffle and Pancake Breakfast Sandwich Recipes

Ham, Egg, Cheese and Buttermilk Pancake Sandwich

Ingredients:

Servings: 1

Cooking Time: 5 minutes

- 2 buttermilk pancakes (leftovers or you can make fresh ones for the recipe)
- 1 egg
- 1 slice of mild cheddar cheese
- 1 slice of ham or Canadian bacon
- 2 tablespoons of maple syrup

Directions:

1. Make sure you take the time to get the breakfast sandwich maker preheating as you assemble the ingredients in the kitchen.
2. Take one of the pancakes, placing in the bottom of your sandwich maker.
3. Top with the slice of the ham or Canadian bacon. Then drizzle the syrup over the ham.
4. Top with the slice of the mild cheddar cheese.
5. Add the egg to the egg pan.
6. Place the remaining pancake in the top slot.
7. Close up the sandwich maker, cooking for five minutes or until the egg has completely finished cooking.
8. Remove the egg pan and then carefully remove the sandwich.
9. Serve warm.

Mediterranean English Muffin

Ingredients:

Servings: 1

**Cooking Time:
5 minutes**

- 1 English muffin, sliced
- 1 tsp. olive oil
- Salt and pepper to taste
- 1 ounce feta cheese crumbled
- 1 roasted red pepper in oil, drained
- 1 slice tomato
- 1 tbsp. basil pesto
- 1 large egg

Directions:

1. Preheat the breakfast sandwich maker.
2. Place half of the English muffin, cut-side up, inside the bottom tray of the sandwich maker.
3. Brush the English muffin with the olive oil and sprinkle with salt and pepper.
4. Top the muffin with the crumbled feta, roasted red pepper and tomato.
5. Slide the egg tray into place and crack the egg into it. Use a fork to stir the egg, just breaking the yolk.
6. Place the second half of the English muffin on top of the egg.
7. Close the sandwich maker and cook for 4 to 5 minutes until the egg is cooked through.
8. Carefully rotate the egg tray out of the sandwich maker then open the sandwich maker.
9. Remove the top English muffin and brush with basil pesto.
10. Replace the English muffin and enjoy your sandwich.

Pineapple, Bacon Waffle Sandwich

Ingredients:

- 8 plain waffles
- 8 slices of bacon, precooked
- 4 slices of sharp cheddar cheese
- 1 - 20 ounce can of slice pineapple, well drained

Directions:

1. Be sure to begin by ensuring your sandwich maker is preheated.
2. Place one waffle in the bottom slot of the appliance.
3. Top with two slices of pineapple.
4. Then, place two slices of bacon on top of the pineapple, covering the bacon with a slice of the sharp cheddar cheese.
5. Add another waffle to the top slot of the breakfast sandwich maker.
6. Cook for 3-4 minutes, or until the cheddar cheese has melted.
7. Repeat with the rest of the waffles.
8. Serve warm and enjoy the different flavors for a filling, fruity, Hawaiian breakfast.

Bagel with Lox Sandwich

Ingredients:

Servings: 1

Cooking Time: 5 minutes

- 1 whole grain bagel, sliced
- 2 ounces smoked salmon
- 2 tbsp. cream cheese
- 1 tsp. minced red onion
- 1 tsp. minced chives
- 1 large egg

Directions:

1. Preheat the breakfast sandwich maker.
2. Place one half of the bagel, cut-side up, inside the bottom tray of the sandwich maker.
3. Top the bagel with smoked salmon.
4. Stir together the cream cheese, red onion and chives then spread over the salmon.
5. Slide the egg tray into place and crack the egg into it. Use a fork to stir the egg, just breaking the yolk.
6. Place the second half of the bagel on top of the egg.
7. Close the sandwich maker and cook for 4 to 5 minutes until the egg is cooked through.
8. Carefully rotate the egg tray out of the sandwich maker then open the sandwich maker to enjoy your sandwich.

Quick and Easy Quesadillas

Servings: 1

Cooking Time: 5 minutes

Ingredients:

- 2 small round tortillas
- 2 slices cooked bacon
- 1 ounce shredded cheddar jack cheese
- 1 tbsp. minced red onion
- 1 tbsp. minced red pepper
- 1 tbsp. BBQ sauce
- 1 large egg
- 1 tbsp. fresh salsa
- 1 tbsp. sour cream

Directions:

1. Preheat the breakfast sandwich maker.
2. Place one of the tortillas inside the bottom tray of the sandwich maker. Brush with BBQ sauce.
3. Break the pieces of bacon in half and place them on top of the tortilla. Sprinkle with cheese, red onion and red pepper.
4. Slide the egg tray into place and crack the egg into it. Use a fork to stir the egg, just breaking the yolk.
5. Place the second tortilla on top of the egg.
6. Close the sandwich maker and cook for 4 to 5 minutes until the egg is cooked through.
7. Carefully rotate the egg tray out of the sandwich maker then open the sandwich maker.
8. Remove the top tortilla and spread with salsa and sour cream. Replace the tortilla and enjoy your sandwich.

Anytime Quesadillas

Ingredients:

- 2 mini Tortillas
- 1 slice Bacon, cooked and crumbled
- 1 ounce white Cheddar cheese, shredded
- 1 tbsp onions, chopped
- 1 tbsp green pepper, chopped
- 1/4 Tbsp butter, (or lite cooking spray if desired)
- Ground cumin, pinch
- Salt to taste
- 1 large egg
- Sour cream (optional)
- Salsa (optional)

Servings: 1

Cooking Time: 5 minutes

Directions:

1. Preheat breakfast sandwich maker.
2. Place one-tortilla into bottom ring of breakfast sandwich maker
3. In small frying pan, melt butter and sauté onions and peppers until soft and translucent; about 3 minutes.
4. In small bowl, whisk eggs with fork. Add sautéed onions and peppers to eggs. Stir in pinch of cumin and salt.
5. Lower cooking plate and top ring. Add egg mixture.
6. Top with remaining tortilla.
7. Close cover. Cook 4 – 5 minutes. Gently rotate cooking plate handle away clockwise. Lift rings. Remove breakfast sandwich with a plastic, nylon or wooden spatula.
8. Optionally top with sour cream and salsa.

Vegan Sausage Sandwich

Ingredients:

Servings: 1

Cooking Time: 5 minutes

- 1 vegan English muffin, sliced
- 1 vegan sausage patty, cooked
- 1 slice Vegan cheese
- 1 ounce firm tofu
- Pinch garlic powder
- Salt and pepper to taste

Directions:

1. Cut the tofu into a circle and sprinkle it with garlic powder, salt and pepper.

2. Heat the oil in a small skillet and add the tofu. Cook for 2 to 3 minutes on each side until lightly browned.

3. Preheat the breakfast sandwich maker.

4. Place half of the English muffin, cut-side up, inside the bottom tray of the sandwich maker.

5. Top the muffin with the sausage patty, vegan cheese and tofu.

6. Place the second half of the English muffin on top of the tofu.

7. Close the sandwich maker and cook for 4 to 5 minutes until heated through.

8. Carefully open the sandwich maker and enjoy your sandwich.

9 781804 462195